REPTIL

KOMODO DRAGONS

By Kathleen Connors

Please visit our website, www.garethstevens.com. For a free color catalog of all our high-quality books, call toll free 1-800-542-2595 or fax 1-877-542-2596.

Library of Congress Cataloging-in-Publication Data
Connors, Kathleen
Komodo dragons / by Kathleen Connors.
cm. – (Really wild reptiles)
Includes bibliographical references and index.
Summary: This book tells about Komodo dragons, the world's largest living lizards, including physical characteristics, habitat, how they raise their young, and their endangered status.
Contents: Real dragons – Look and se– – Wanted dead or alive – A poisonous end – Deadly bite – Happy home? – Mates and mothers – Babies in danger! – So few remain.
ISBN 978-1-4339-8380-1 (pbk.)
ISBN 978-1-4339-8381-8 (6-pack)
ISBN 978-1-4339-8379-5 (hard bound) –
1. Komodo dragon—Juvenile literature [1. Komodo dragon 2. Lizards]
I. Title 2013
597.95/968

First Edition

Published in 2013 by
Gareth Stevens Publishing
111 East 14th Street, Suite 349
New York, NY 10003

Designer: Sarah Liddell
Editor: Kristen Rajczak

Photo credits: Cover, p. 1 Khoroshunova Olga/Shutterstock.com; pp. 5, 9, 20 Uryadnikov Sergey/Shutterstock.com; p. 7 Pius Lee/Shutterstock.com; p. 11 CORDIER Sylvain/hemis.fr/Getty Images; p. 13 © iStockphoto.com/AYImages; p. 15 Christy Liem/Shutterstock.com; p. 17 Kevin Lings/Shutterstock.com; p. 19 W K Fletcher/Photo Researchers/Getty Images; p. 21 G Tipene/Shutterstock.com.

Printed in the United States of America

CPSIA compliance information: Batch #CW13GS: For further information contact Gareth Stevens, New York, New York at 1-800-542-2595.

Contents

Words in the glossary appear in **bold** type the first time they are used in the text.

REAL DRAGONS

Until about 100 years ago, scientists weren't sure Komodo dragons even existed. They can be found only on Komodo Island and other islands in the Lesser Sunda Islands, which are part of Indonesia. That's less than 390 square miles (1,000 sq km) of land!

Komodo dragons are the largest living lizards. They can reach 10 feet (3 m) long and weigh more than 300 pounds (136 kg). While these huge lizards don't breathe fire like dragons in stories, they're still pretty wild.

Komodo dragons have been known to swim between islands looking for food.

LOOK AND SEE

Komodo dragons have a small, flat head and four short legs. Their heavy-looking body ends with a thick tail. Like other **reptiles**, Komodo dragons are covered in scales. They're commonly red, gray, or black.

Komodo dragons don't have strong hearing or see well at night. However, they have a sharp sense of smell. They use their long, forked tongue to smell, much like a snake does. By "tasting" the air, they can even tell from which direction a smell is coming!

Komodo dragons use their sense of smell to find food.

What a Wild Life!

Komodo dragons' sense of smell is so good, they can smell **carrion** from miles away!

WANTED DEAD OR ALIVE

What does a Komodo dragon eat? Just about anything! Komodo dragons are carnivores, or meat eaters. They hunt small deer, pigs, snakes, and fish. They're also noted for eating carrion. But they eat more than an animal's meat. Komodo dragons are known to eat their **prey's** bones, hooves, fur, and guts!

Komodo dragons are **patient** hunters. They may hide in the brush for hours before prey comes by. Even then, Komodo dragons might attack an animal and let it get away!

A Komodo dragon can eat as much as 80 percent of its weight in one meal.

A POISONOUS END

Komodo dragons won't go hungry if their prey gets away. That's because an animal won't get very far if a dragon has bitten it.

Komodo dragons are **venomous**. Their venom mixes with spit as they bite and tear at their prey. After being attacked by a Komodo dragon, prey may live anywhere from hours to a few more days. However long it takes, Komodo dragons use their sense of smell to follow the weakened prey. Then, dinner is served!

What a Wild Life!

Komodo dragons may seem scary, but they actually spend a lot of time laying in the sun and sleeping.

Komodo dragons often share their prey with other nearby dragons.

DEADLY BITE

Komodo dragons use their sharp teeth and claws to attack animal prey. You don't want to find yourself near a Komodo dragon either! They're dangerous to people, too.

The teeth of a Komodo dragon are somewhat like many sharks' teeth. They're serrated, or have a uneven, zigzag edge like a knife. A Komodo dragon's mouth is full of **bacteria**, too. Until scientists discovered the dragon's venom, they thought these bacteria caused prey to die after a Komodo dragon attack.

A Komodo dragon uses its teeth and claws as well as its venom to wound prey.

HAPPY HOME?

On the Lesser Sunda Islands, there are **volcanoes** and, for a short part of the year, terrible rainstorms. The rest of the time, there's little water on the islands, and it's very hot. But Komodo dragons seem to like their home. Scientists think they've lived there for millions of years!

Komodo dragons can be found in many places on the islands—from forests to beaches. To escape the heat, they dig holes in the ground called burrows. They may have more than one burrow in their territory.

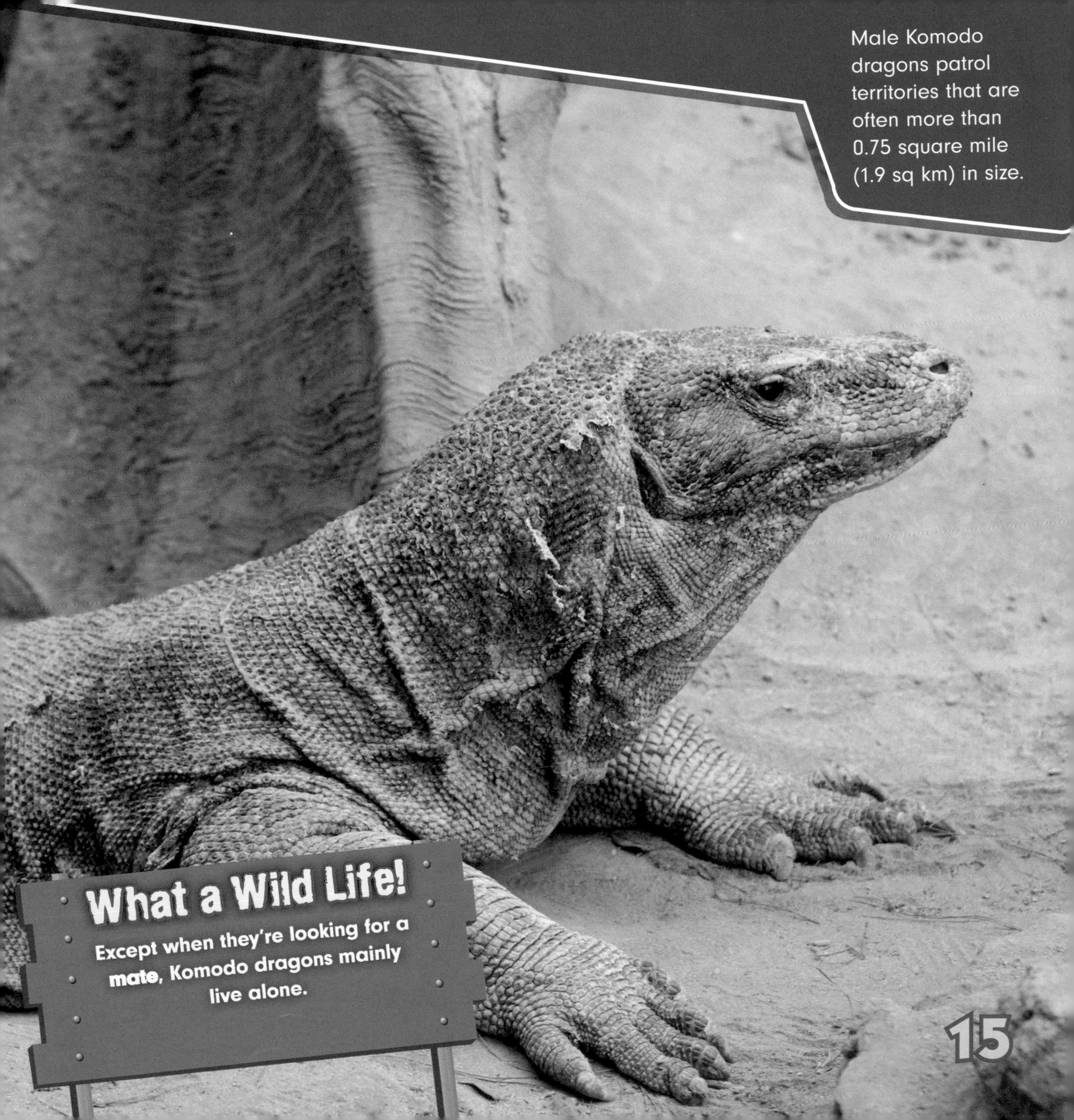

Male Komodo dragons patrol territories that are often more than 0.75 square mile (1.9 sq km) in size.

What a Wild Life!

Except when they're looking for a **mate**, Komodo dragons mainly live alone.

MATES AND MOTHERS

When looking for a mate, male Komodo dragons sometimes stand on their back legs and tail, and fight each other with their front legs. The loser either lays still or runs away, while the winner claims his mate.

A female Komodo dragon lays about 30 eggs. Sometimes she digs a shallow nest for them. Often, a female Komodo dragon lays her eggs in the nest of a local turkey! Then, she may lay on the eggs until they hatch about 9 months later.

What a Wild Life!

There are four times as many male Komodo dragons as females in the wild.

Though a mother Komodo dragon may guard her eggs, she doesn't help her babies once they've hatched.

BABIES IN DANGER!

Baby Komodo dragons may be more than a foot (30 cm) long when they hatch. Even though that's bigger than adult lizards of other **species**, these babies aren't safe. In fact, they're hunted by adult Komodo dragons!

Soon after hatching, baby Komodo dragons climb trees to keep away from older, hungry Komodo dragons. They stay in the trees eating bugs, small lizards, and birds' eggs until they're big enough to try living on the ground.

About 10 percent of an adult Komodo dragon's food is made up of baby Komodo dragons.

What a Wild Life!

Komodo dragon venom doesn't harm other Komodo dragons.

SO FEW REMAIN

There are so few Komodo dragons left that these large lizards are an **endangered** species. Today, only about 3,000 to 5,000 Komodo dragons live on the Lesser Sunda Islands.

Since 1980, most of the islands have been part of Komodo National Park. Komodo dragons are supposed to be safe within the park, though sometimes people still hunt them illegally. But people aren't the only danger. Because their population is so small, Komodo dragons could die out from illness, loss of prey, or one of the island's volcanoes.

Many scientists and zoos around the world are trying to keep the Komodo dragon species alive for years to come.

King of the Lizards

Komodo dragons have many wild features that help them catch their prey.

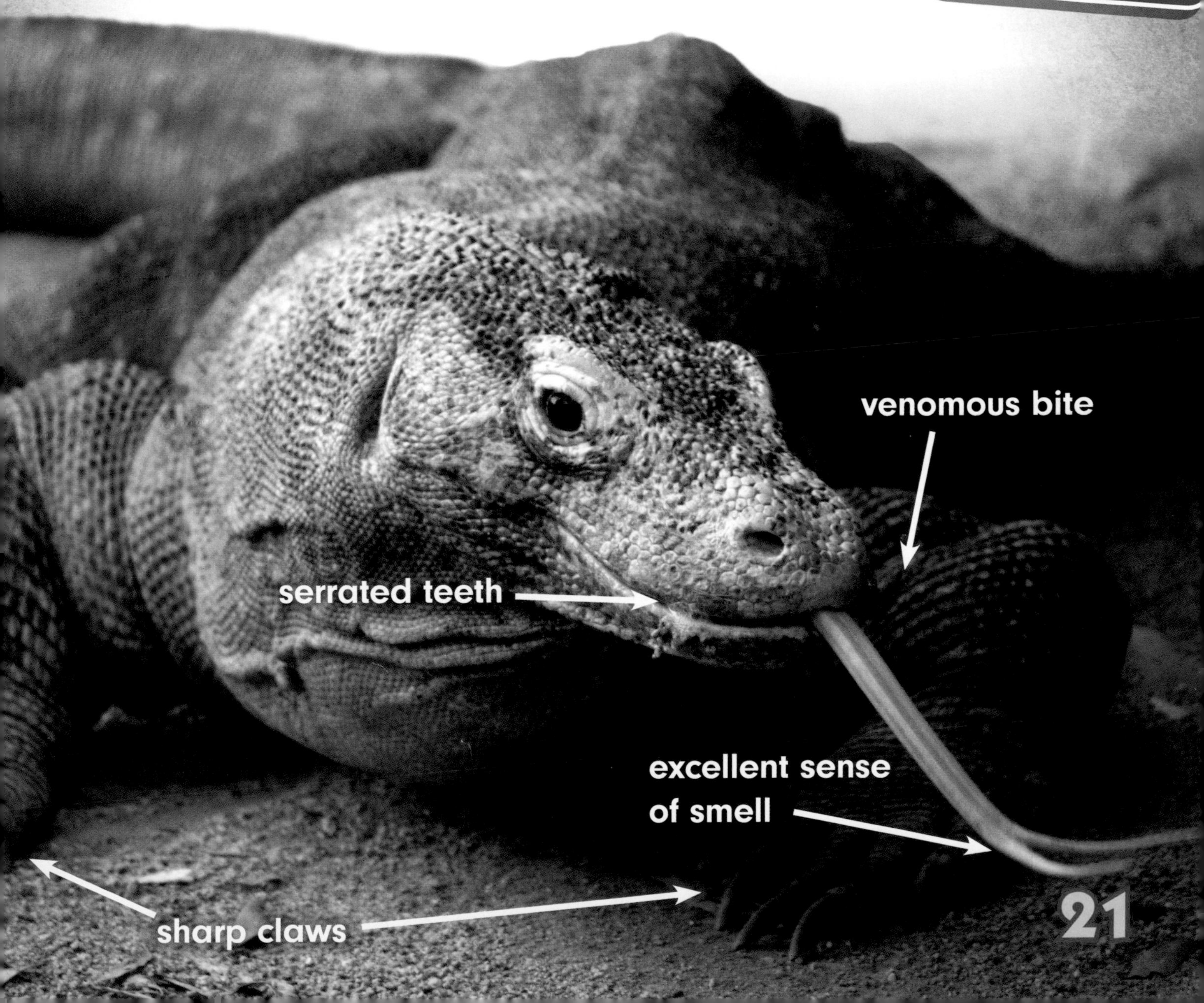

venomous bite

serrated teeth

excellent sense of smell

sharp claws

GLOSSARY

bacteria: tiny creatures that can only be seen with a microscope

carrion: a dead, rotting animal

endangered: in danger of dying out

mate: one of two animals that come together to produce babies

patient: able to wait a long time

prey: an animal that is hunted by other animals for food

reptile: an animal covered with scales or plates that breathes air, has a backbone, and lays eggs, such as a turtle, snake, lizard, or crocodile

species: a group of animals that are all of the same kind

venomous: able to produce a liquid called venom that is harmful to other animals

volcano: an opening in a planet's surface through which hot, liquid rock sometimes flows

FOR MORE INFORMATION

Books

Crump, Marty. *Mysteries of the Komodo Dragon: The Biggest, Deadliest Lizard Gives Up Its Secrets*. Honesdale, PA: Boyds Mills Press, 2010.

Thomas, Isabel. *Remarkable Reptiles*. Chicago, IL: Raintree Publishing, 2013.

Websites

Komodo Dragon
animal.discovery.com/reptiles/komodo-dragon/
Watch Komodo dragons in action in the many videos on this website.

Reptiles: Komodo Dragon
www.sandiegozoo.org/animalbytes/t-komodo.html
Read all about the Komodo dragon and see many pictures.

INDEX